HAL•LEONARD

JAZZ PLAY ALONG

Book and CD for B♭, E♭ and C Instruments

volume
57

Arranged and Produced
by Mark Taylor

VINCE GUARALDI
10 FAVORITE TUNES

T0085235

BOOK

CD

Photo by William "PoPsie" Randolph
www.PoPsiePhotos.com

ISBN 978-1-4234-0128-5

HAL•LEONARD®
CORPORATION
7777 W. BLUEMOUND RD. P.O. BOX 13819 MILWAUKEE, WI 53213

Visit Hal Leonard Online at
www.halleonard.com

Vince Guaraldi

Volume 57

Arranged and Produced by
Mark Taylor

Featured Players:

Graham Breedlove–Trumpet
John Desalme–Saxophones
Tony Nalker–Piano
Jim Roberts–Bass
Steve Fidyk–Drums

Recorded at Bias Studios, Springfield, Virginia
Bob Dawson, Engineer

HOW TO USE THE CD:

Each song has <u>two</u> tracks:

1) Split Track/Melody

Woodwind, Brass, Keyboard, and **Mallet Players** can use this track as a learning tool for melody style and inflection.

Bass Players can learn and perform with this track – remove the recorded bass track by turning down the volume on the LEFT channel.

Keyboard and **Guitar Players** can learn and perform with this track – remove the recorded piano part by turning down the volume on the RIGHT channel.

2) Full Stereo Track

Soloists or **Groups** can learn and perform with this accompaniment track with the RHYTHM SECTION only.

CD
1 : SPLIT TRACK/MELODY
2 : FULL STEREO TRACK

BLUE CHARLIE BROWN

BY VINCE GUARALDI

C VERSION

MED. SWING

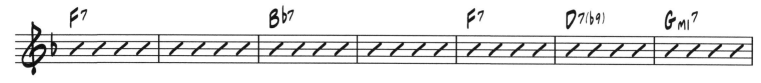

CHRISTMAS TIME IS HERE

WORDS BY LEE MENDELSON
MUSIC BY VINCE GUARALDI

C VERSION

CD

◆ **5** : SPLIT TRACK/MELODY
◆ **6** : FULL STEREO TRACK

C VERSION

FRIEDA
(WITH THE NATURALLY CURLY HAIR)

BY VINCE GUARALDI

FINE

* SOLOS (2 FULL CHORUSES)

F6   D7   Gmi7   C7   Ami7   D7   Gmi7   C7   F7   Bb7   B07

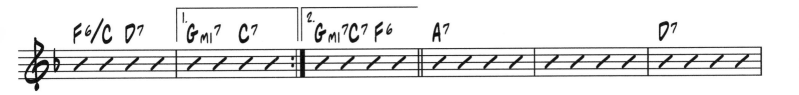

F6/C   D7 |1. Gmi7   C7 ||2. Gmi7 C7 F6   A7   D7

G7   Gmi7   C7

F6   D7   Gmi7   C7   Ami7   D7   Gmi7   C7   F7

D.S. AL FINE
TAKE REPEAT

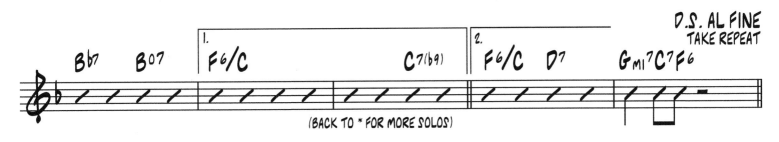

Bb7   B07 |1. F6/C   C7(b9) ||2. F6/C   D7   Gmi7 C7 F6

(BACK TO * FOR MORE SOLOS)

CD

◆ **7** : SPLIT TRACK/MELODY
◆ **8** : FULL STEREO TRACK

C VERSION

THE GREAT PUMPKIN WALTZ

BY VINCE GUARALDI

MED. JAZZ WALTZ

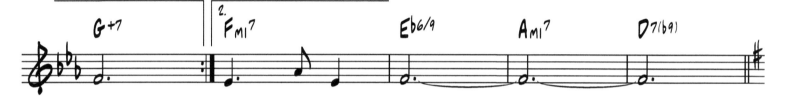

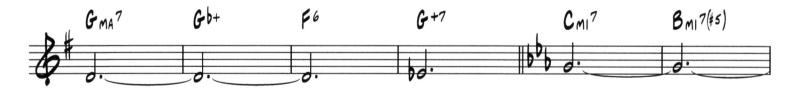

TO CODA ⊕

SOLO
C$_{mi7}$ | B$_{mi7(\#5)}$ | B$\flat_{mi7}$ | E$\flat^7$ | F/A

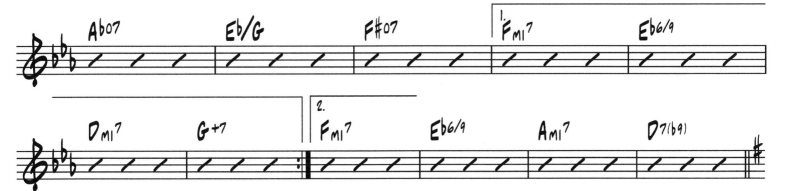

A$\flat^{o7}$ | E$\flat$/G | F$\#^{o7}$ | 1. F$_{mi7}$ | E$\flat^{6/9}$

D$_{mi7}$ | G^{+7} | 2. F$_{mi7}$ | E$\flat^{6/9}$ | A$_{mi7}$ | D$^{7(\flat9)}$

G$_{MA7}$ | | C$_{mi(MA7)}$ C$_{mi}^6$ | G$_{MA7}$ | G$_{MA7}$

C$_{mi(MA7)}$ | C$_{mi}^6$ | G$_{MA7}$ | | C$_{mi(MA7)}$ | C$_{mi}^6$

G$_{MA7}$ | G$\flat^+$ | F^6 | G^{+7} | C$_{mi7}$ | B$_{mi7(\#5)}$

B$\flat_{mi7}$ | E$\flat^7$ | F/A | A$\flat^{o7}$ | E$\flat$/G

F$\#^{o7}$ | F$_{mi7}$ | E$\flat^{6/9}$ | D$_{mi7}$ | G^{+7} D.C. AL CODA TAKE REPEAT

CODA
E$\flat^{6/9}$/B$\flat$ E$\flat^{6/9}$ | F$_{mi7}$ | E$\flat^{6/9}$ | E$\flat^{6/9}$/B$\flat$ | 1. E$\flat^{6/9}$ | 2. E$\flat^{6/9}$

HAPPINESS THEME

BY VINCE GUARALDI

C VERSION   JAZZ BALLAD

LINUS AND LUCY

CD
11 : SPLIT TRACK/MELODY
12 : FULL STEREO TRACK

BY VINCE GUARALDI

C VERSION

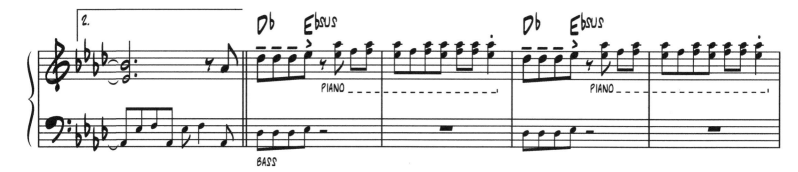

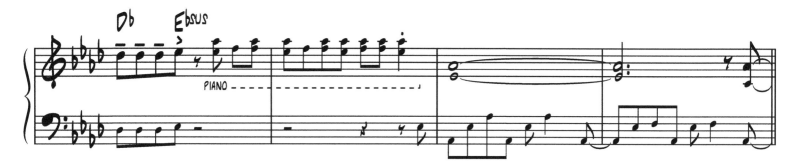

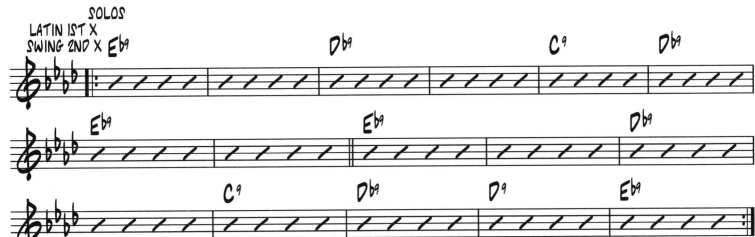

SOLOS

LATIN 1ST X
SWING 2ND X

OH, GOOD GRIEF

BY VINCE GUARALDI

C VERSION

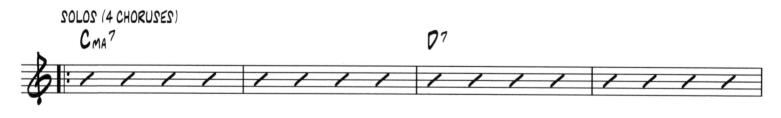

THE PEBBLE BEACH THEME

BY VINCE GUARALDI

CD
◆ 15 : SPLIT TRACK/MELODY
◆ 16 : FULL STEREO TRACK

C VERSION

SAMBA

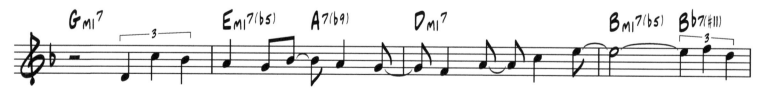

SKATING

BY VINCE GUARALDI

C VERSION

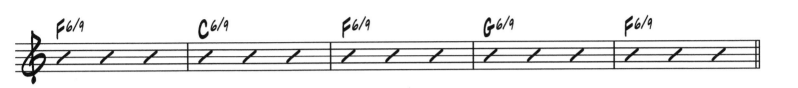

Surfin' Snoopy

BY VINCE GUARALDI

C VERSION

Blue Charlie Brown

CD
1: SPLIT TRACK/MELODY
2: FULL STEREO TRACK

BY VINCE GUARALDI

Bb VERSION

MED. SWING

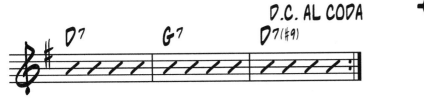

CD

③ : SPLIT TRACK/MELODY
④ : FULL STEREO TRACK

CHRISTMAS TIME IS HERE

WORDS BY LEE MENDELSON
MUSIC BY VINCE GUARALDI

B♭ VERSION

SURFIN' SNOOPY

BY VINCE GUARALDI

CD
- **19**: SPLIT TRACK/MELODY
- **20**: FULL STEREO TRACK

Bb VERSION

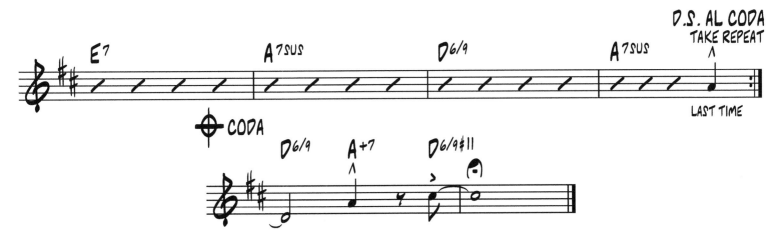

FRIEDA
(WITH THE NATURALLY CURLY HAIR)

BY VINCE GUARALDI

FINE

* SOLOS (2 FULL CHORUSES)

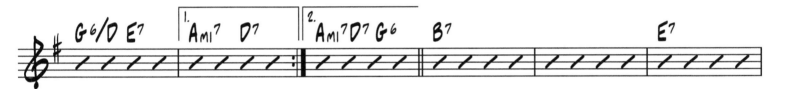

D.S. AL FINE
TAKE REPEAT

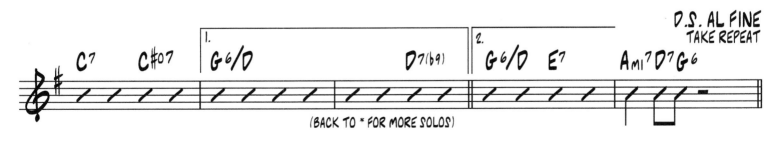

(BACK TO * FOR MORE SOLOS)

THE GREAT PUMPKIN WALTZ

BY VINCE GUARALDI

SOLO

D.C. AL CODA
TAKE REPEAT

CD
◆ 9 : SPLIT TRACK/MELODY
◆ 10 : FULL STEREO TRACK

HAPPINESS THEME

BY VINCE GUARALDI

B♭ VERSION

JAZZ BALLAD

29

SOLO

D.S. AL CODA

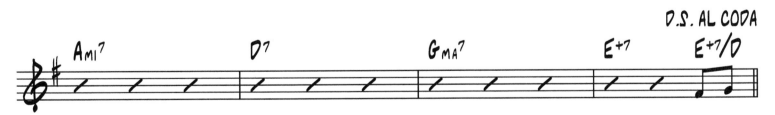

LINUS AND LUCY

BY VINCE GUARALDI

B♭ VERSION

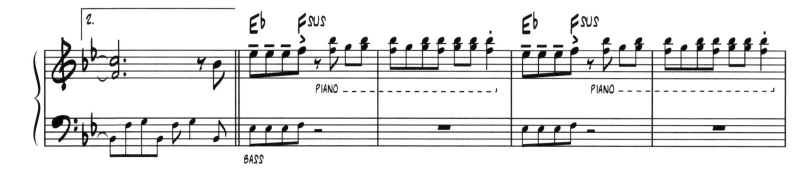

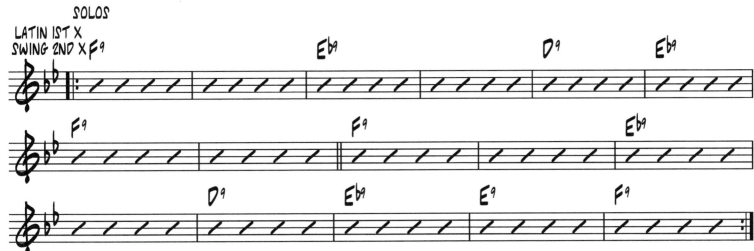

TO CODA ⊕

SOLOS

LATIN 1ST X
SWING 2ND X F⁹   E♭⁹   D⁹   E♭⁹

F⁹   F⁹   E♭⁹

D⁹   E♭⁹   E⁹   F⁹

D.S. AL CODA
TAKE REPEAT   ⊕ CODA

OH, GOOD GRIEF

BY VINCE GUARALDI

Bb VERSION

CD

◆**15** : SPLIT TRACK/MELODY
◆**16** : FULL STEREO TRACK

THE PEBBLE BEACH THEME

BY VINCE GUARALDI

B♭ VERSION SAMBA

SOLOS (3 CHORUSES)

D.C. AL CODA

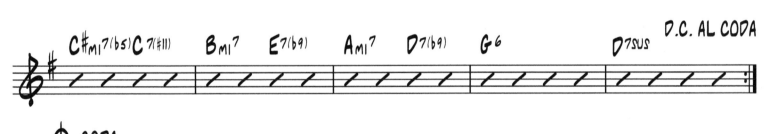

CODA

PLAY 3 TIMES

SKATING

BY VINCE GUARALDI

BLUE CHARLIE BROWN

BY VINCE GUARALDI

E♭ VERSION

CHRISTMAS TIME IS HERE

CD
3 : SPLIT TRACK/MELODY
4 : FULL STEREO TRACK

WORDS BY LEE MENDELSON
MUSIC BY VINCE GUARALDI

Eb VERSION

FRIEDA
(WITH THE NATURALLY CURLY HAIR)

BY VINCE GUARALDI

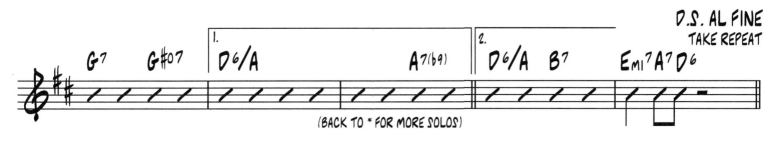

THE GREAT PUMPKIN WALTZ

BY VINCE GUARALDI

E♭ VERSION

MED. JAZZ WALTZ

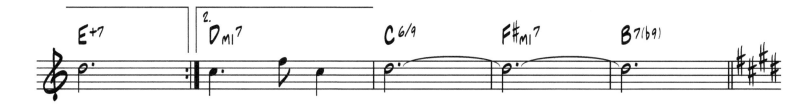

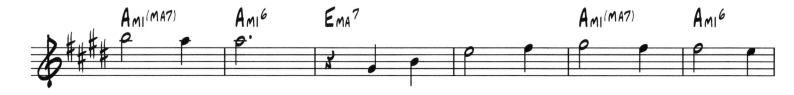

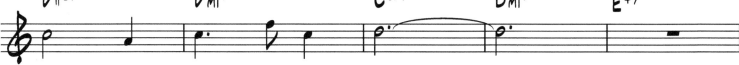

SOLO

Am17   G#m17(#5)   Gm17   C7   D/F#

F07   C/E   D#07   1. Dm17   C6/9

Bm17   E+7   2. Dm17   C6/9   F#m17   B7(b9)

Ema7   Am1(MA7)   Am16   Ema7

Am1(MA7)   Am16   Ema7   Am1(MA7)   Am16

Ema7   Eb+   D6   E+7   Am17   G#m17(#5)

Gm17   C7   D/F#   F07   C/E

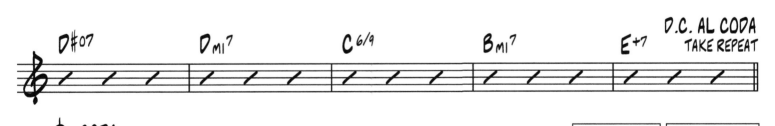

D#07   Dm17   C6/9   Bm17   E+7   D.C. AL CODA TAKE REPEAT

CODA

C6/9/G   C6/9   Dm17   C6/9   C6/9/G   1. C6/9   2. C6/9

CD

◆ 9 : SPLIT TRACK/MELODY
◆ 10 : FULL STEREO TRACK

HAPPINESS THEME

BY VINCE GUARALDI

E♭ VERSION   JAZZ BALLAD

SOLO

D.S. AL CODA

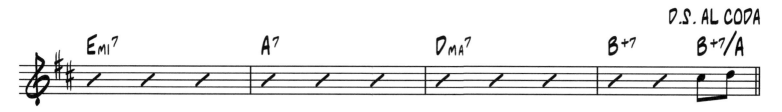

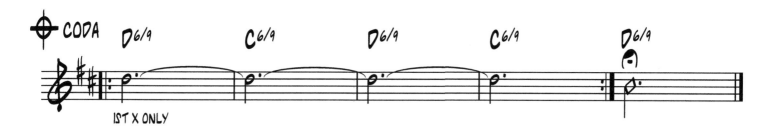

LINUS AND LUCY

BY VINCE GUARALDI

E♭ VERSION

STRAIGHT
N.C.

TO CODA ⊕

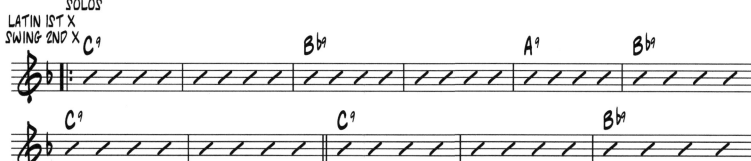

SOLOS
LATIN IST X
SWING 2ND X

D.S. AL CODA
TAKE REPEAT

⊕ CODA

OH, GOOD GRIEF

BY VINCE GUARALDI

Eb VERSION

49

THE PEBBLE BEACH THEME

BY VINCE GUARALDI

E♭ VERSION

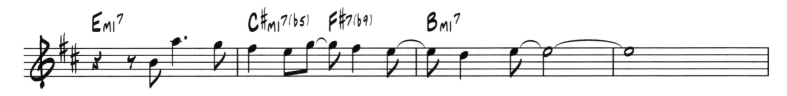

SKATING

BY VINCE GUARALDI

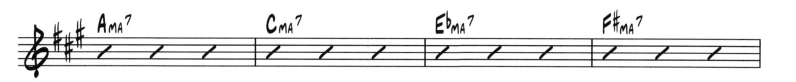

SURFIN' SNOOPY

BY VINCE GUARALDI

Blue Charlie Brown

BY VINCE GUARALDI

CD
1 : SPLIT TRACK/MELODY
2 : FULL STEREO TRACK

𝄢 C VERSION

CHRISTMAS TIME IS HERE

WORDS BY LEE MENDELSON
MUSIC BY VINCE GUARALDI

SURFIN' SNOOPY

BY VINCE GUARALDI

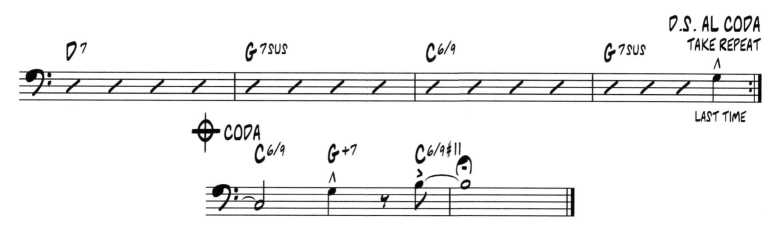

FRIEDA
(WITH THE NATURALLY CURLY HAIR)

BY VINCE GUARALDI

FINE

* SOLOS (2 FULL CHORUSES)

(BACK TO * FOR MORE SOLOS)

D.S. AL FINE
TAKE REPEAT

CD

7: SPLIT TRACK/MELODY
8: FULL STEREO TRACK

THE GREAT PUMPKIN WALTZ

BY VINCE GUARALDI

9: C VERSION

MED. JAZZ WALTZ

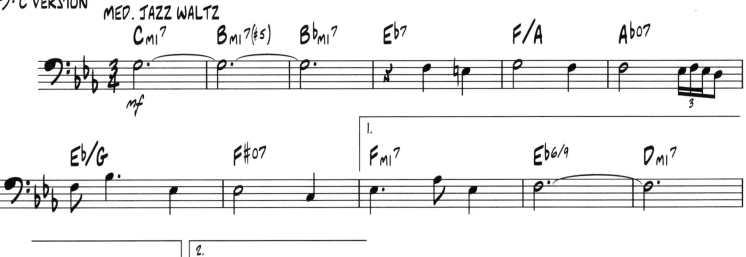

TO CODA

SOLO

D.C. AL CODA
TAKE REPEAT

HAPPINESS THEME

BY VINCE GUARALDI

🎵: C VERSION

JAZZ BALLAD

SOLO

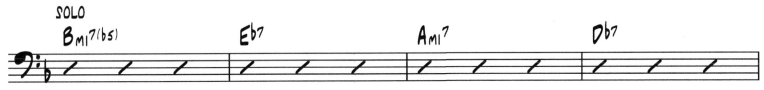

D.S. AL CODA

CODA

1ST X ONLY

LINUS AND LUCY

BY VINCE GUARALDI

𝄢: C VERSION

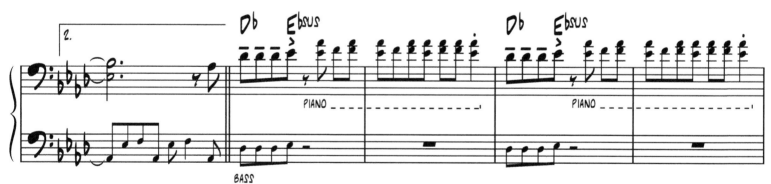

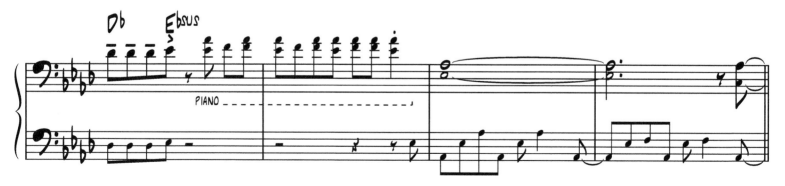

TO CODA ⊕

SOLOS
LATIN 1ST X
SWING 2ND X $E\flat 9$ $D\flat 9$ $C9$ $D\flat 9$

$E\flat 9$ $E\flat 9$ $D\flat 9$

$C9$ $D\flat 9$ $D9$ $E\flat 9$

D.S. AL CODA
TAKE REPEAT   ⊕ CODA

CD

: SPLIT TRACK/MELODY
: FULL STEREO TRACK

OH, GOOD GRIEF

BY VINCE GUARALDI

𝄢: C VERSION

SOLOS (4 CHORUSES)

CD

15 : SPLIT TRACK/MELODY
16 : FULL STEREO TRACK

THE PEBBLE BEACH THEME

BY VINCE GUARALDI

𝄢: C VERSION

SAMBA

SKATING

BY VINCE GUARALDI

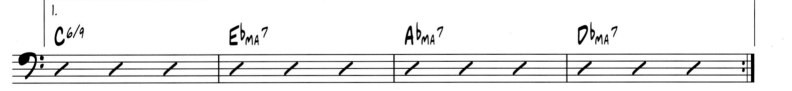

For use with all B-flat, E-flat, Bass Clef and C instruments, the **Jazz Play-Along Series** is the ultimate learning tool for all jazz musicians. With musician-friendly lead sheets, melody cues, and other split-track choices on the included audio, these first-of-a-kind packages help you master improvisation while playing some of the greatest tunes of all time.

FOR STUDY, each tune includes a split track with: melody cue with proper style and inflection • professional rhythm tracks • choruses for soloing • removable bass part • removable piano part.

FOR PERFORMANCE, each tune also has: an additional full stereo accompaniment track (no melody) • additional choruses for soloing.

To see full descriptions of all the books in the series, visit: